Original title:
The Glow of Evergreen Dreams

Copyright © 2024 Creative Arts Management OÜ
All rights reserved.

Author: Juliette Kensington
ISBN HARDBACK: 978-9916-94-386-1
ISBN PAPERBACK: 978-9916-94-387-8

Echoing Dreams in the Heart of the Forest

In the woods where squirrels play,
They dance and sing all day.
Beneath the trees, they make a mess,
Flying acorns, what a test!

One tree's face is full of glee,
A laughing log, you have to see.
With each step, a twig will crack,
Then off they go, up the track.

The raccoons wear hats and ties,
Hosting parties under the skies.
With moonlight cakes and silly cheers,
They spread delight throughout the years.

The owls hoot jokes, quite absurd,
In their world, it's never blurred.
With every giggle, echoes soar,
In the forest, we laugh for more.

Echoes of Green Serenity

In a forest of mismatched socks,
Where trees wear hats and dance like flocks,
The squirrels hold a raucous ball,
While raccoons try to impress us all.

The owls hoot, but can't quite rhyme,
Chasing echoes in their own time,
With giggles from the sleepy bees,
And jokes hidden behind the leaves.

Flickering Shadows of Dreams

A shadow pranced, a funny sight,
Tap-dancing under the moon's light,
The dreams rolled in like clumsy skates,
Bumping into trees with giddy rates.

The clouds cheered on, with grumbling glee,
As night creatures joined in the spree,
With laughter that shakes the starlit sky,
While nightingales croon a comic goodbye.

Moonlit Canopy of Hope

Beneath the moon, the critters yawn,
A raccoon sneezes, while playing dawn,
A giggle slips from ferny lips,
As fireflies begin their odd little trips.

The porcupine sports a fancy tie,
Swapping stories with the nearby pie,
Among the leaves, such silly dreams,
Where laughter ripples through silver streams.

Shimmering Leaves in Silent Night

Leaves chat quietly, a whispering crowd,
Cracking jokes, making spirits proud,
The stars poke fun at their own shine,
Bolting through the cosmos like a grapevine.

A bumblebee buzzes with crazy glee,
Painting the night with silliness free,
Under the shimmer of the leafy chat,
Where dreams giggle in a soft little hat.

A Symphony of Green and Glow

In the forest, trees wear crowns,
With squirrels dancing, no one frowns.
A symphony of chirps and tweets,
As mushrooms pull on tiny feets.

Branches sway with playful grace,
While cheeky rabbits join the race.
The mushrooms giggle, make a scene,
In this vibrant woodland green!

Reflections of Hope in Leafy Dreams

Upon a leaf, a snail does glide,
Chasing dreams, quite unoccupied.
A ladybug, with polka dots,
Says 'What's up?' and scurries lots.

The flowers hum a merry tune,
While bees buzz 'round like little balloons.
With each petal, a silly cheer,
In this land of laughter, oh so dear!

Harvesting Light from the Woods

In the woods, the sunlight plays,
Tickling leaves in funny ways.
A bear in shades, sitting quite still,
Sipping honey, what a thrill!

The raccoons form a conga line,
While frogs croak jokes, oh so fine!
With every chuckle, shadows blend,
In the light, where laughter bends.

Enchanted Greenery and Celestial Glow

In gardens bright, the gnomes conspire,
To roast marshmallows by the fire.
Fairies giggle, make some noise,
As rabbits show off their new toys.

The vines twist around like spaghetti,
While snails slip-slide, all quite sweaty.
The moon chuckles, lighting the show,
In enchanted greenery, what a glow!

Echoes of Dreams in Verdant Valleys

In valleys green where laughter sings,
A squirrel juggles acorn rings.
The birds in trees crack silly jokes,
While deer dance round in feathered coats.

The sun peeks through in playful darts,
A breeze that tickles all our hearts.
A wildwood party, join the scene,
As goats wear hats, they're rather keen!

Luminous Tapestry of Woodlands

In woods so bright, where wild things shout,
A hedgehog starts a conga rout.
The foxes laugh and dance so free,
While owls refute their nightly spree.

With vines that twist and leaves that sway,
We trip and tumble in our play.
A raccoon sports a quirky tie,
And all the trees just wonder why!

Silver Streams within the Emerald Wilderness

The bubbling brook makes silly sounds,
While frogs in coats make silly bounds.
A fish that fishes for a laugh,
As turtles ponder, 'What's the math?'

The dragonflies wear tiny hats,
While beavers sing, "Just chat, chat, chat!"
In waters bright, the fun runs wild,
As laughter echoes, pure and mild.

Dappled Light on a Bed of Moss

Upon the moss, we lounge and dream,
Where mushrooms burst with laughter's beam.
With sunlight jazzing through the leaves,
A giggling fox just never grieves.

The mushrooms pirouette so bold,
And ants all march in lines of gold.
In nature's realm, where joy's the king,
We find the fun in every fling!

Whispers of Timeless Woods

In a forest where squirrels wear hats,
And owls spin tales of friendly chats.
The trees crack jokes with creaky limbs,
While hidden frogs perform their whims.

The mushrooms dance in polka dots,
While hedgehogs sing in merry spots.
The sunlight tickles each leaf's face,
As bunnies hop with a silly grace.

With pinecone hats and acorn shoes,
The rabbits play their favorite blues.
The breeze hums tunes with giggly notes,
While critters plan their playful quotes.

In this grove, laughter is the norm,
Where nature thrives and joy is warm.
So gather 'round for a chuckle spree,
In the woods where fun flows wild and free.

Luminous Pines at Dusk

Beneath the arms of tall, bright trees,
Where raccoons sip on berry teas.
The twilight brings a glow so bold,
As fireflies weave their tales of gold.

With whispers sweet and riddles fair,
The foxes plot with cheeky flair.
They roll in leaves, creating fun,
While stars peek through, one by one.

The porcupines strut in their best gear,
Making friends with a judge, the deer.
Each branch above holds giggles tight,
As night unfolds its twinkling light.

In these woods where laughter thrives,
The playful spirit truly dives.
Join the jesters, it's quite a show,
In the glow of night, let humor flow.

Beneath a Canopy of Stars

In the stillness where shadows prance,
The raccoons plan their midnight dance.
With twinkling lights, they spin around,
As laughter echoes, joyous sound.

The turtles wear their party hats,
While fireflies buzz like tiny bats.
Each leafy branch holds secrets shared,
And every chuckle shows we cared.

The owls provide the perfect beat,
As crickets strum from their cozy seat.
The stars above wink in delight,
At woodland antics throughout the night.

In this realm of cheer and jest,
The woodland's heart feels truly blessed.
So raise a toast with dew-drop cheer,
To the shining dreams that bring us near.

Radiance Within the Woodland Heart

Within the woods where laughter calls,
The chipmunks chase their fuzzy balls.
They tumble down from trees so high,
As giggles burst like popcorn, oh my!

The snails wear shades in the morning sun,
Sipping on dew—life's so much fun!
While busy bees throw a picnic treat,
In this garden, every day's a feat.

The pines sway softly, sharing jokes,
Joining in, the gentle oaks.
With stories told from bark to leaf,
In every laugh, we find relief.

So gather 'round, the night is bright,
With woodland magic, pure delight.
Embrace the joy in every part,
For laughter lights the woodland heart.

Shades of Radiance and Nature's Heart

In the forest, trees wear hats,
Squirrels dance while chatting rats.
Mossy carpets, dreams unite,
Chasing shadows, what a sight!

Frogs in tuxes sing their tune,
Underneath the curious moon.
Leaves like tiny parachutes,
Catch the giggles, funny roots.

Bunnies jump, they play charades,
Tickling ferns on joyful blades.
Nature's heart beats wild and free,
In a world of pure glee!

Starry Nights in Mossy Glades

A hedgehog wears a tiny crown,
While owls laugh and never frown.
Fireflies twinkle, take a dive,
In this place, we feel alive!

Badgers bake in secret nooks,
Whiskers twitch with quirky looks.
Moonlight serves the funniest pies,
To squirrels with their silly ties.

Dancing shadows spin and sway,
As night-time creatures laugh and play.
In the glades beneath the stars,
Even stones can thrive like czars!

Glimmering Dreams Beneath Ancient Cedars

Cedars whisper ancient tales,
While pixies ride on snailish trails.
Crazy giggles fill the air,
As critters leap without a care.

Wandering through the ferny maze,
Finding treasures in the haze.
The moon takes selfies, bright and bold,
Of mysteries that never get old.

Raccoons in pajamas, what a sight,
Holding dance parties through the night.
With a waltz that spins quite free,
Embracing every oddity!

Viridescent Fantasies in the Moonlight

Green hats for gnomes in the mist,
While rabbits plan their bucket list.
Singing flowers, quite profound,
Breathe in laughter all around.

Treetop giggles touch the sky,
As crickets join, no need to shy.
At midnight, owls wear their specs,
Debating life while chasing flecks.

Chippy squirrels, acorns high,
Make a joyful ruckus, oh my!
In this world, wild dreams take flight,
Under the stars, it's pure delight!

Light Play in the Woodland Realm

In the woods where squirrels dance,
A rabbit's hat tricks cause a glance.
Trees wear crowns of leafy flair,
Laughter echoes in the air.

Bouncing beams in playful jest,
Nature's jokes are simply the best.
Acorns fall like tiny drums,
As chipmunks march and gather crumbs.

A spider's web shines like a prize,
While butterflies perform in disguise.
The mossy floor is soft and rich,
Where every shadow plays a glitch.

So if you're feeling quite a mess,
Head to the woods for some distress.
Giggles sparkle in the glade,
As woodland wonders serenade.

Illuminated Reveries Beneath the Boughs

Under branches thick and wide,
The mushrooms giggle, they won't hide.
Fairies toss their shimmering dust,
While old owls snore, it's simply a must.

The moonlight winks, a sly old chap,
While rabbits munch in a moonlit nap.
Witty shadows prance in glee,
As crickets sing their symphony.

A hedgehog dons a tiny cape,
While other critters plot escape.
The glowworms twinkle, a starry crew,
In jest, they glow just for you.

So take a stroll, enjoy the show,
Where laughter's bright, it's all aglow.
In this realm of whimsy and light,
Join the fun until the night.

Secrets of the Luminous Grove

In a grove where secrets lie,
Frogs tell tales as they leap high.
The trees chuckle, sharing hacks,
While raccoons plot their midnight snacks.

Twinkling lights dance on the ground,
Every cranny, giggles resound.
Squirrels juggling acorn treats,
With lively music, the forest greets.

A fox in glasses reads a book,
As owls wink from their lofty nook.
The breeze has secrets, it loves to share,
Of funny antics happening there.

So wander far, let laughter bloom,
In this enchanted, quirky room.
Each moment glows, a jest indeed,
Nature's humor is all we need.

Dreamscapes in the Forest Shade

Beneath the shade of leafy dreams,
The forest giggles, or so it seems.
With every twist in old tree roots,
A parade of funny woodland hoots.

Here, the fairies tease the gnomes,
Who trip on toadstools, miss their homes.
Bunny boogies, spins about,
It's hard to hold in all the shout.

A raccoon wearing a tiny tie,
Sips on juice while the owls fly by.
The sunlight filters through the leaves,
Where laughter floats, and nothing grieves.

So join the fun, don't hesitate,
In this forest, laughter's fate.
Let dreams unfurl in this bright shade,
And cherish each whimsical escapade.

Warmth of Leaves Under a Starlit Sky

Under the stars, the leaves all smile,
They whisper secrets in a leafy style.
A squirrel pirouettes, quite the dancer,
While birds gossip like they're at a Lancer.

Moonlight tickles the branches low,
Leaves blush in the night, putting on a show.
Each rustle is laughter, each shadow a jest,
Nature's comedy club, oh, we're so blessed!

Secret Gardens of Luminous Paths

In a garden where giggles bloom quite loud,
Worms wear top hats; they're so very proud.
Rabbits are jesters, with antics galore,
Each petal a punchline we can't ignore.

Daisies make crowns for the bumblebee king,
Butterflies flutter, oh what joy they bring!
A cucumber plays banjo, just for a laugh,
While carrots all gather to photograph!

Embracing Eternity in Nature's Embrace

Under the trees, where the clovers sing,
A snail in a hat claims to be the king.
The flowers are prancing, oh what a scene,
A dance of wild creatures, all in between.

The old oak chuckles, "I've seen it all,"
While ferns gossip under nature's call.
A chipmunk recites poetry, quite divine,
As laughter wraps round like a vintage vine.

Dappled Ambitions Beneath Towering Giants

In the shade of giants with arms spread wide,
A crafty cat plot, oh, what a wild ride!
Acorns roll by in a hilarious race,
While leaves chortle softly; it's quite a place.

The bumblebees buzz with tales far and near,
As mushrooms debate on their favorite cheer.
Here, laughter unfolds in whispers and beams,
Life's grandest circus ignites all our dreams.

Bright Visions in the Depth of Eden

In the garden where socks go to hide,
Cabbages dance with unbridled pride.
Bananas play chess with the cherry trees,
While radishes giggle in the summer breeze.

A squirrel's wearing a sunhat so bright,
As daisies debate if it's day or night.
The roses sing songs with a dash of flair,
While the tulips gossip without a care.

Glowing Trails of a Verdant Odyssey

On paths where the wild mushrooms twirl with grace,
The hedgehogs march at a comical pace.
With shoes made of leaves and hats of moss,
Every critter's a king, they won't take a loss.

In fields of kale, they throw a grand ball,
Donning outfits of nature, they're having a ball.
Lettuce leads laughter, while carrots do prance,
In this vibrant realm, the veggies dance!

Midnight Musings Among Evergreen Shadows

Beneath the stars, the trees share a joke,
With whispers of pine and a lens of smoke.
The owls wink twice, and the fireflies cheer,
While bushes crack up at the sound of a deer.

A raccoon in pajamas steals cookies at night,
In a moonlit caper, it's quite a sight.
The shadows are giggling, they bounce and play,
In this woodland night, all cares drift away.

Dreams Embroidered with Nature's Palette

Colors collide where dreams take flight,
As daisies don hats that are ridiculously bright.
Crickets compose with a pizzicato sound,
While oranges tumble from trees all around.

The clouds are like candy, sweet on their own,
With honeycomb sunshine that's widely known.
A parade of bananas waltzes in style,
As nature's palette, they bring a big smile.

Fables of Light and Leaf

In the woods where shadows play,
A squirrel juggles nuts all day.
While rabbits sip their minty brew,
They laugh at trees in silly shoes.

The birds compose a cackling song,
About a moose who thinks he's strong.
He tried to play a game of fetch,
With fish who say, "We're not your pets!"

A fox tells tales of fancied fame,
And brags about his daring game.
But when he trips on roots so wide,
He finds himself a laughing slide.

Beneath the boughs the creatures cheer,
Their humor echoes bright and clear.
In this realm of whimsy and glee,
Nature spins its fables free.

Harmonies of Nature's Brilliant Tones

A catbird chirps in silly tune,
While raccoons dance beneath the moon.
The owls spin tales with such delight,
They scare themselves with their own fright!

The frogs compose a croaky rap,
While turtles go for nature's nap.
A chorus blooms from every nook,
With lyrics sprung from every brook.

A woodpecker drums a funky beat,
While daisies sway on nimble feet.
In every laugh and chirp so bright,
Nature's humor lights the night.

Thus, in this woodland symphony,
Lies laughter wrapped in harmony.
Each creature plays its joyful part,
In nature's concert, full of heart.

Illumination through Twisted Vines

Twisted vines with a wink and twist,
Tangle up a silly gist.
They whisper secrets, play hide and seek,
As fireflies dance, without a peek.

A chameleon dons a polka dot,
While frogs decide to try a trot.
The sun peeks through with a sunny grin,
As critters join the fun and spin.

Vines tickle leaves in silly fights,
While bugs proclaim their daring flights.
A lizard slides on a leafy groove,
As shadows shift and start to move.

Each twist and turn in this green maze,
Leads to laughter, sparks, and rays.
In a garden where time flies by,
Every giggle reaches the sky.

Reflections in a Calm, Leafy Pool

A pond reflects a silly frog,
Attempting to leap on a dog.
It jumps with flair, a smirk so wide,
Only to land with a splash and glide.

Nearby, the fish giggle and flip,
As turtles join the laughter trip.
The reeds bend low to catch the sound,
Of chortles echoing all around.

The water ripples with every joke,
As dragonflies give a little poke.
The scene unfolds in gleeful array,
Where every creature finds a way.

In this pool of fun, reflections shine,
With rippling laughter, so divine.
In calm waters, joy finds its place,
As nature enjoys its playful grace.

Nature's Embrace in Soft Glow

In the woods where squirrels dance,
Beneath the leaves, they take a chance.
A chipmunk in a tiny hat,
Sips on tea, and chats with a cat.

Mushrooms giggle, growing low,
With fairy lights that flash and glow.
The rabbits hop, they think they're cool,
While wise old owls act like fools.

Among the trees, a laughter spree,
As pinecones roll, so wild and free.
A bear who sings off-key at night,
To fireflies that blink with delight.

So come and join this silly scene,
Where nature plays, and life's a dream.
With every leaf and twig that sways,
You'll find the joy in nature's ways.

Nightfall's Embrace Amongst Evergreens.

As shadows stretch and night unfolds,
A raccoon winks and proudly scolds.
The stars above begin to tease,
While crickets chirp with utmost ease.

A hedgehog rolls, a tumble here,
With laughter echoing loud and clear.
The moon it whispers, "Come and play,"
While owls plan pranks, by night, by day.

In every corner of the wood,
A game of hide-and-seek is good.
With pine trees swaying, mischief wakes,
And every creature giggles and quakes.

So dance beneath that silver sheen,
Let joy arise, let laughter preen.
For in the night, we find our fun,
Amongst the evergreens, we run.

Whispers of Verdant Wishes

In the meadow, wishes roam,
A butterfly makes flowers home.
They whisper secrets on the air,
While rabbits strike a funny dare.

A hedgehog dons a flowery suit,
Stepping lightly on tiny roots.
In the grass, a game they play,
Who can hop the dreamiest way?

With dandelions, blow the seeds,
As critters gather, sharing deeds.
The ants parade in crazy lines,
While frogs compose their wacky rhymes.

So join the whispers, let them flow,
With leafy laughter, watch it grow.
In every shade and vivid beam,
Life's just a silly, endless dream.

Luminescence in Leafy Echoes

In the forest's leafy arms,
A glowworm hums with tiny charms.
Beneath the boughs, a party brews,
As raccoons dance in neon shoes.

Sassy squirrels trade acorn jokes,
While frogs make funny little pokes.
A laughing tree starts to sway,
With every twist, it steals the day.

The air is thick with giggles bright,
As fireflies twirl in sheer delight.
Beneath the stars, we twist and shout,
In every heart, there is no doubt.

So come and bask in joy tonight,
With nature's humor, pure and right.
Let leafy echoes guide your dreams,
In woodland fun, or so it seems.

Radiance Beneath the Canopy

In the woods where critters roam,
Squirrels dance like they own a throne.
The sun tickles the leaves up high,
While birds try to sing, but just squeak and cry.

Mossy stones play hide-and-seek,
With mushrooms giggling, oh so meek.
A rabbit donning a tiny hat,
Waves to the fox who's busy at that!

Under the boughs, a feast of cheer,
Ice cream cones for the deer, oh dear!
The trees whisper jokes only they know,
As the breeze joins in, putting on a show!

So if you wander where that path winds,
Bring your laughter, leave worries behind.
For in this realm of the slightly absurd,
Nature's humor is always preferred.

Dreams Woven in Green Hues

A frog in a tux, how dapper he looks,
Imagining plots from old storybooks.
The owl in spectacles, wise as can be,
Gives fashion advice to a dancing tree.

Pine cones fall, but not with grace,
One hit a chipmunk, what a funny face!
They laugh and tumble, oh what a sight,
Nature's comedy show, pure delight!

The brook gurgles with jokes so slick,
While flowers giggle at bees with a flick.
The snails have a race, oh what a slow pace,
Yet cheer for each other, no hint of disgrace.

Clouds drift by, imagining the scene,
A stage set for laughter, so nice and serene.
With dreams in their hearts like bright green hues,
This forest's a place for whimsical views!

Ethereal Light Among the Pines

Where the pines grow tall and sway,
Laughter echoes, brightens the day.
A hedgehog plays on a swing of vine,
While the sunbeams giggle, oh so divine!

Bunnies hop in a conga line,
With witty quips that truly shine.
A gopher juggles acorns with flair,
While turtles cheer from their comfy chair.

Fireflies buzz with a dazzling show,
Dancing around like they're in a disco.
Bark beetles beat to the rhythm of fun,
In this light-hearted world, joy's never done!

So wander where giggles twine and spin,
In the warm embrace of all that's been.
For under the pines, with laughter so bright,
Life is a carnival, pure and light!

Shimmering Shadows of the Forest

In shadows green, where secrets dwell,
A raccoon's prank brings laughter as well.
The ferns sway like they've had too much tea,
As squirrels plot a ruckus, oh what glee!

The sun's rays peek through, all shy and coy,
While mushrooms mimic a rave with joy.
Bunny bands playing tiny guitars,
Singing to the rhythm of twinkling stars.

Amid the shimmering, shadows dance,
A snail spins tales, given half a chance.
With every croak, the frogs take a bow,
Creating a spectacle—come see it now!

So lay down your worries, join in the jest,
Let the warmth of the forest help you rest.
For here in the glades, life's simply a dream,
Where laughter sparkles like a bright moonbeam!

Murmurs of Serenity Among Sturdy Roots

Beneath the trees, a whisper flows, A squirrel scolds in comical prose. The roots hold stories, deep and wide, Where mushrooms gather in giddy pride.

Laughter crackles like twigs in glee, As ants host picnics, oh so free. A chipmunk dances, with nuts in tow, In dreams of grandeur, like a grand show.

Branches wave like overzealous fans, Cheering for critters in funny plans. A raccoon plots a heist at dusk, Sneaking snacks with a mask of husk.

The wind joins in, a chuckling friend, As nature's circus seems to extend. Under sturdy roots, in leafy beams, Whispered joys bloom in silly dreams.

Shaded Echoes of Daydreams

In shady nooks, a snail takes flight, Dreaming of races at the speed of light. Grasshoppers giggle, crafting a tune, While frogs croon ballads beneath the moon.

A playful breeze, it tickles the leaves, Causing the branches to dance as they weave. A squirrel in shades, adorned like a king, Shouts out loud, 'Watch me swing!'

Caterpillars lounge with snacks in hand, Preparing for parties, oh isn't it grand? Ants scurry 'round, a bustling parade, With tiny top hats in lustrous jade.

Reflections flutter, a comedic race, In nature's theatre, a light-hearted space. Each echo whispers, a jest to redeem, As shadows wobble in daytime gleam.

Flickering Light in the Embrace of Trees

Under the boughs, lights start to blink, Fireflies flash as they waltz and sink. A wise old owl with spectacles tight, Reviews the antics, such a funny sight.

Mice play poker, with acorns assigned, Betting their cheese, oh how they're blind! The crickets chirp, their rhythms askew, In a symphony of chuckles and goo.

A squirrel in reindeer horns does a jig, Prancing with flair, oh so big! The shadows laugh, they tumble and roll, In this tranquil space, they play a whole.

Beneath the constellations, bright and wide, A skunk shares jokes, a fragrant guide. Flickering laughs in a woodland stream, Where everyone basks in a whimsical dream.

Timeless Reflections in Evergreen Glades

In the glades where the shadows play, A fox tells tales of mischief and sway. Leaves rustle softly, joining the jest, As nature guffaws, feeling quite blessed.

A tortoise brags of races so slow, Claiming the crown, 'I'm the star of the show!' With every stretch, a laugh does escape, While rabbits hop by in a playful shape.

The mossy floor is a dance hall divine, Where mushrooms twirl, and the sunlight shines. Each step a giggle, each turn a cheer, In timeless moments that bring good cheer.

As past meets present, the laughter expands, Nature's own humor written in strands. In reflections that shimmer and beam with delight, The glades are alive with joy and light.

Wanderlust in the Lush Embrace

In a forest deep, where snacks abound,
Squirrels hold parties, nuts scattered 'round.
Beneath leafy hats, they wiggle and prance,
Trying to charm, the trees take a chance.

Mossy carpets trade secrets with the breeze,
While chipmunks debate the best climbing trees.
Mushrooms wear hats like peculiar glee,
They giggle at nature's oddity spree.

Birds in a choir, they sing in a flap,
Wishing for acorns instead of a nap.
Frogs pull their pranks, in the dusk they croak,
Each croak a jest, oh what a joke!

As shadows dance on this leafy stage,
Creatures perform in nature's grand page.
With every mishap, they burst into cheer,
In this wild world, laughter's crystal clear.

Radiant Palettes of the Forest Floor

In a patch of sunlight, fairies prepare,
Dancing with daisies, twirling in air.
A raccoon debates with a feisty old crow,
Who gets the last snack? Oh, what a show!

Wildflowers giggle in colors so bright,
Debating if daisies or poppies are right.
A butterfly winks, which way does it go?
It flutters past mushrooms, putting on a show.

A hedgehog with glasses reads mossy old tales,
Of epic adventures, and warty snails' trails.
"Once I was brave, king of the hill!"
The others all chuckle, "You, brave? What a thrill!"

From shadows and sunlight, the forest does hum,
In a tapestry woven, the fun is no crumb.
Every twinkling leaf is a laugh waiting there,
Whispering secrets, all floating in air.

Elusive Light in the Depths of Nature

Glowworms are hiding in dark, twisty caves,
Making up stories of daring brave knaves.
"Have you seen my sandwich?" a badger will cry,
While fireflies giggle, "Now don't you be shy!"

Toadstools are benches for frogs who will sing,
A chorus of croaks for the joy that they bring.
Some mushrooms wear shirts with polka-dot flair,
While drumming to nature, they have quite a care.

A rabbit on stilts hops high in a twirl,
Challenging squirrels in a soft wooded whirl.
"Who says I can't dance?" the rabbit then shouts,
And the whole forest giggles in joyful sprout.

As twilight descends, with stars shining bright,
Creatures of whimsy will dance through the night.
In shadows and giggles, the woods hum with cheer,
Under the moon, laughter's always near.

Secrets Hidden Beneath Formations of Green

Beneath leafy giants, a ruckus is found,
Gnomes with their maps, plotting mischief around.
With a wink and a laugh, they scheme on their quests,
To steal all the acorns, put squirrels to tests.

Raccoons in masks hold a midnight feast,
With cookies and berries, they munch at the least.
A gopher joins in with a spoon in each paw,
Balancing snacks with an excited guffaw!

A wise old owl chuckles, "Watch those raccoons!"
While ants in a line belt out silly tunes.
Their backpacks are heavy with snacks so sublime,
But dancing in circles, they've run out of time!

With secrets and giggles, the forest is bright,
Where laughter is whispered beneath moonlit light.
In this marvel of green, where funny things blend,
Nature's joyful chorus will never quite end.

Light and Life in Leafy Groves

Beneath the branches, squirrels play,
Chasing shadows, bright and gay.
A raccoon laughs, what a sight!
He steals a snack, then takes flight.

In the grass, bugs dance and hum,
Wiggle and giggle, here they come!
A frog in shades, what a cool dude,
Winks at the sun, in a carefree mood.

A tree stump hosts a tea party grand,
With mushrooms as chairs, the guests take a stand.
The owl serves up jokes, so witty and slick,
While the rabbits split sides with their hop and their kick.

Then as dusk wraps its soft curtain,
The critters pack up, but are certain,
Tomorrow they'll meet in laughter and gleam,
In the heart of the forest, where all things seem.

Wandering Through Glimmers of Green

In a forest of giggles, I stomp and I bounce,
With flowers that tickle and roots that pounce.
A butterfly flutters, in polka-dot flair,
As I trip over vines, with not a single care.

The sunlight dances on leaves of bright hue,
While squirrels make jokes about why they can't chew.
I chuckle at moss, so long and so fuzzy,
Its fashion sense, well, it's just a bit fuzzy.

A hedgehog stumbles, takes a wild spin,
He rolls like a ball and lets out a grin.
A rabbit complains that his carrot is too small,
But hey, it's the thought, and we're having a ball.

As shadows grow longer, the laughter still rings,
With crickets as backup, they join in to sing.
Through the glimmers of green, with friends all around,
We wander through joy, where fun can be found.

Tranquility Beneath Shimmering Canopies

Under the boughs, the calmness sets in,
Where a gnome gives a wink and a rodent's a twin.
A snail on a trail, oh what a grand race,
It's slowpoke Olympics, a smile on each face.

The breeze tells a joke through the rustling leaves,
While tree limbs wave back, in playful reprieves.
A wise old owl nods, with a twinkle in eye,
While all the wee folk just giggle nearby.

A pond ripples softly, mirroring delight,
As frogs pull their hop-stops, leaping left and right.
Each splash is a chuckle, a celebration wide,
Beneath shimmering shadows, where silliness hides.

With shadows now stretching, we bid adieu,
The laughter still dancing, so lively and true.
In the heart of the grove, peace sparkles and beams,
With tranquility finding us in fluffy dreams.

The Serenity of Sunlit Pines

In sunlight's embrace, the pines start to sway,
While chipmunks debate how to dance through the day.
A woodpecker drums out a beat in the bark,
While fireflies twinkle, igniting the park.

Comically solemn, a bunny does pose,
Striking silly selfies with blossoms and bows.
Oh, how the sunlight makes shadows leap high,
As a lizard rolls over to sunbathe nearby.

The clouds overhead play hide and seek,
While squirrels snack freely, no time to be meek.
Their chatter erupts in a chorus of cheer,
As we frolic and fret without any fear.

In moments of peace, we burst out in giggles,
Swaying beneath pines, doing funny wiggles.
So here in the warmth of nature's delight,
We find hilarity under the sun's golden light.

Celestial Reflections in Nature's Heart

In a forest where the critters tease,
A squirrel tried yoga, fell down with ease.
The butterflies giggled as they fluttered near,
While a wise old owl waved, 'Come join my cheer!'

Moonlight winks from each branch and root,
A rabbit's ambition? To dance in a suit!
Frogs croak a tune, they're the band of the night,
While fireflies flash like they're out to ignite!

Little hedgehogs roll, thinking they're slick,
But tripping over mushrooms, they plop and they stick.
A party of whiskers, they tumble and bounce,
Until a wise tortoise says, 'Just don't pounce!'

Stars peep down, with a twinkle or two,
And the pine trees sway like they're feeling the groove.
The night air is filled with laughter and glee,
As nature's own circus puts on quite a spree!

Luminescence of Life's Enchantment

In a meadow where daisies sway to the hum,
A ladybug sings, 'Come dance, everyone!'
The bees in big hats buzz low to the ground,
Creating sweet tunes, such a humorous sound!

Crickets with jokes make the night seem so bright,
While the stars, they chuckle, throwing sparks of light.
A wiggly worm spins around in a show,
Said, 'I'm the star, come on, don't be slow!'

Bouncing bunnies with oversized shoes,
Trading their carrots for sparkly blues.
A tiny green lizard, a comedian bold,
Cracks up the crowd with stories retold.

As the moonbeams giggle across every hill,
A raspberry bush shouts, 'I'm yielding my fill!'
Dreams of bright fruits in the laughing night air,
Make this wild garden a truly rare fair!

Wistful Nights Beneath Verdant Boughs

Underneath a tree, where shadows play tricks,
A raccoon holds court, juggling with sticks.
The owls in their wisdom begin to debate,
'This nut is the best! Wait, just try this plate!'

The whispers of leaves carry secrets so sweet,
Chipmunks are gossiping, close by the creek.
A playful breeze swoops, causing a stir,
Filling the air with ridiculous blur!

Fireflies wear glasses, what a sight to behold,
Claiming they've read every book ever told.
The pine tree bobbles its head with delight,
Saying, 'Join the party; we're dancing tonight!'

With laughter and whimsy, the forest alive,
Every creature, a friend, in this magical hive.
The moon beams down, a cheeky little mouse,
Squeaks, 'Life is a circus in our leafy house!'

Stardust Among the Evergreens

At the base of a pine, where the shadows do creep,
A fox paints his whiskers, saying, 'Don't weep!'
The night critters gather, their spirits alight,
As they share silly tales and take quite a flight.

Squirrels declare themselves royalty here,
While a frog croaks a tune that brings the deer near.
With twirls and flips, they dance on the ground,
In a forest of laughter, community found.

The moon giggles softly, its light like a wink,
As animals ponder the next missing link.
'Tomorrow we'll feast on the tastiest leaves,'
Says a raccoon in glasses, earning a tease!

With whispers of stardust in each playful breeze,
They join in a circle, wild saucy with ease.
In the realm of the trees, where the joy never ends,
Life's deliciously funny, on nature, depends!

Dreams in the Breath of Pines

In the forest, I had a whim,
To dance with squirrels on a limb.
They chuckled as I tripped and swayed,
While pinecones rained, a grand parade.

A rabbit winked, a fox just grinned,
As I claimed victory, unpinned.
"Who knew trees could be so wise?"
I told my jokes, they rolled their eyes.

A raccoon laughed, he stashed a nut,
Said, "In this game, you're quite the cut!"
I bowed to cheers from bushes wide,
My silly moves, their forest pride.

With dreams aloft, I shouted loud,
"To all my friends, I'm brave, unbowed!"
The pines just rustled, shyly stared,
As mushrooms chuckled, slightly bared.

Glowing Secrets of Forest Depths

In moonlit glades where shadows play,
A frog recites jokes in his bay.
The owls hoot laughter, wide-eyed glee,
As fireflies dance like a wild spree.

"Why did the pine tree feel so great?"
"Because it found its true mate!"
Giggling mocks from branches tall,
A gust of wind makes laughter call.

The turtles slow, they hear the jest,
"Who needs speed when you have zest?"
In these woods, we cheer for fun,
As beams of light outshine the sun.

The shadows twist, they clap and shout,
As critters cheer, they have no doubt.
That even trees, with bark and skin,
Share glowing secrets deep within.

Illuminated Paths in Whispering Pines

Along the path where whispers hum,
The rabbits gossip, swatting crumbs.
The wise old crow, with tales to tell,
Mocks my shoes—"You've tripped quite well!"

"Dance like no one's judging you!
Even the trees would join in too!"
I leapt and spun, the squirrels squeaked,
While laughter echoed, lightly tweaked.

A hedgehog joined, with wobbly glee,
Said, "I'll roll if you roll with me!"
We tumbled down the pine-strewn lane,
While giggles brewed like summer rain.

At dusk, the stars began to peek,
They winked and waved—oh, what a sneak!
In pine-scented air, we danced and pranced,
A merry scene, all dreams enhanced.

Twinkling Tales of the Old Grove

In the grove where shadows play tricks,
A bear did stand, who juggled sticks.
With laughter loud, the tree trunks swayed,
As visions of jokes in moonlight played.

"Why do pinecones never get lost?"
"Because they always know the cost!"
The birds whistled, their tunes so bright,
As the stars blinked back in sheer delight.

The groundhogs giggled, rolled in delight,
"Let's host a dance under the light!"
Footfalls soft upon the mossy floor,
The night unfolded, laughter galore.

With stories spun of dreams so wide,
The old grove's heart, forever tied.
In twinkles and chirps, our night took flight,
A woodland romp till morning light.

Serene Echoes of Nature's Light

In a forest dressed in green,
Squirrels dance, a silly scene.
The trees giggle, branches sway,
Nature's joke, come out and play.

A raccoon wears a hat too grand,
While rabbits hop in marching band.
The flowers buzz with laughter, too,
As bees perform a disco view.

The brook hums tunes of glee and cheer,
While frogs in tuxes croak, oh dear!
A butterfly flutters with a wink,
And all the trees just stop and think.

So join the fun and don't be shy,
In this happy wood, let spirits fly.
A world of whimsy waits for you,
Just listen close; it might come true.

Ethereal Trip through Verdant Realms

Through valleys lush with giggles sweet,
The mushrooms dance on little feet.
Fairies chime with laughter bright,
As shadows play in dappled light.

A deer in polka dots prances round,
While butterflies change colors sound.
Jump in puddles filled with cheer,
Even the mud seems to want to steer!

Owl in spectacles reads a book,
While the tables are set with a lovely nook.
The picnic ants tiptoe on their treat,
In this dream, nothing's incomplete.

So roam where giggles greet your way,
In this whimsical nature play.
A slice of joy in every stream,
Living inside a funny dream.

Vivid Illusions of the Wooded Realm

In a woodchuck's cap, a genius lies,
While squirrels plot their nutty ties.
A hedgehog hosts a fancy ball,
With acorns rolling, none can stall.

The leaves whisper secrets, loud yet sweet,
As rabbits juggle carrots on two feet.
A fox in shades takes a cool stance,
While chipmunks join in a wild dance.

Clouds above wear fuzzy hats,
As raccoons laugh at silly chats.
A tree throws shade with a witty sigh,
While sunlight prances, oh me, oh my!

So take a trip through this vibrant scene,
Where every critter's a joyful queen.
Each giggle echoes, pure delight,
In this wood where dreams take flight.

Illuminated Whispers in Nature's Keep

Beneath the stars, the critters play,
The moonlight leads a dance ballet.
An owl hoots jokes from high above,
While shadows wiggle and twirl with love.

A beaver wearing tiny shoes,
Tells tales of rivers, funny views.
While dancing flowers bloom with flair,
And squirrels leap without a care.

The breezes carry playful sighs,
As ladybugs wear bow ties.
Each branch cracks with a giggling sound,
In this lit world, joy's profound.

So wander here, let laughter bloom,
Among the trees, dispelling gloom.
Nature whispers, soft and sweet,
In this secret realm, life's a treat.

Ethereal Paths Through Emerald Groves

In the woods, trees wear green hats,
Squirrels dance like acrobats.
Mushrooms giggle, they're quite the sight,
As rabbits bounce, full of delight.

The babbling brook sings silly tunes,
While bears hum to the light of moons.
A hedgehog trips, gets stuck in a lace,
Oh, what a silly, charming space!

Fluffy clouds float, trying to tease,
While butterflies chase the buzzing bees.
Every critter dons a grin so wide,
In this forest, laughter's our guide.

So take a step on this frolicsome path,
Where nature's humor sparks a hearty laugh.
Every leaf whispers its cheeky jest,
In these emerald groves, life's simply the best!

Vibrant Hues of Hope in the Forest Air

Sunshine sprinkles colors around,
While foxes play tag on the ground.
There's a rainbow in every tree,
Nature smiles, cheerful and free.

A tree stump wears a floppy hat,
While ants march by in a quirky spat.
A bear makes friends with a bright blue jay,
Causing giggles throughout the day.

Dancing leaves join in the tune,
Now twirling under the afternoon.
Each flower blooms with a funny grin,
As chubby bunnies hop right in.

So stomp your feet on this laughter trail,
Where joy and whimsy never fail.
In this vibrant air, let your heart sway,
With giggles and snickers come what may!

Enchanted Twilight in Leafy Whispers

As twilight falls, the fireflies play,
Their flickering lights lead the way.
Owls wear glasses, reading the night,
While frogs croak jokes, oh, what a sight!

Leaves giggle, tickling the breeze,
A raccoon juggles acorns with ease.
Under the stars, mischief unfolds,
With tales of adventure, all proudly told.

Mice wear capes and fly through the dark,
Chasing shadows with a joyful spark.
While trees sway and join the jest,
In this twilight, we're truly blessed.

So stroll through the night and embrace the fun,
Where laughter echoes, and dreams run.
Among leafy whispers, we boldly gleam,
In the heart of laughter, we live the dream!

Crystals of Light in Forest Dreams

Morning dew glistens like tiny gems,
While sprightly foxes lead merry hems.
A snail races, slow but spry,
While bubbles float up to the sky.

The trees trade secrets behind closed bark,
One tells jokes that hit the mark.
Silly shadows play hide and seek,
While the chatty crickets start to squeak.

A parade of rabbits hops down the lane,
While the sun giggles, teasing the rain.
Every petal bursts with laughter bright,
In this magical place, everything's light.

So uncover these crystals, let's laugh anew,
With whispers of joy that feel like dew.
In the depths of the forest, oh what a gleam,
Life is a canvas, painting a dream!

Dance of the Fireflies in Foliage

In the woods where critters play,
Fireflies dance at the end of the day.
They twirl and spin with glee,
Lighting up the evening spree.

A squirrel tried to join the fun,
But tripped and fell; oh what a run!
The glow bugs giggled, sparked and flew,
While hedgehogs cheered, 'You'll get it too!'

The green leaves sway in a silent cheer,
As to the rhythm, we draw near.
A moonlit soirée, laughter all around,
With oddities only nature found.

And as we prance with silly ease,
We hope the bear's asleep, if you please!
But don't you fret, it's all in jest,
For laughter's light, we know, is best!

Serenity Under a Canopy of Dreams

Beneath the branches, shadows dance,
The sun pours down its golden chance.
Bugs chatter, gossiping in the breeze,
While squirrels barter acorns like fees.

A duck quacks out a giggling tune,
While rabbits hop to the beat of the moon.
With a cloud as soft as a marshmallow,
They bounce around, feeling oh-so-fellow.

Oh! What joy in the great outdoors,
Nature's wit, it truly soars.
And when a frog croaks out a joke,
We all can't help but laugh till we choke.

So in this space, our hearts combine,
To hug the sunshine, we feel divine.
With grassy pillows underneath our heads,
We dream of pastries and cozy beds!

Embracing the Essence of Nature's Light

Sunlight trickles through the trees,
The butterflies dance with the bees.
In the meadow, it's a playful sight,
Where every flower feels just right.

A rabbit sneezes, oh how it hops,
While a lazy turtle spins and plops.
The wind whispers softly, 'Chill and groove,'
As nature shakes her way to prove.

Through dandelions, we chase the breeze,
With every giggle, we feel at ease.
The bees get dizzy but don't mind the fuss,
Buzzing 'round in a joyful rush.

Though clouds may gather and drizzle may fall,
We'll dance in puddles, oh, we'll have a ball!
With each splash and laugh, we'll surely ignite,
The essence of fun, pure and bright!

Radiant Journeys through the Timberland

On a path where the wild things roam,
We embark to find our evergreen home.
Where the owls tell tales and pinecones chime,
Every step leaves echoes of laughter in time.

A bear walks by in a fancy hat,
Waving hello to the curious cat.
They giggle and beckon us from afar,
To join their jam beneath the stars.

Raccoons play tricks with mischievous eyes,
As fireflies buzz with their lovely lies.
In every nook, surprises await,
A game of hide and seek with fate.

So off we dance on this radiant quest,
In nature's arms, we feel so blessed.
Let's skate with skunks and shout hooray,
As we relish the beauty of this playful day!

Glimmers of Hope in the Green Dreamscape

In a forest where squirrels dare,
Frogs in tuxedos dance without care.
Trees giggle, whisper, twist in the breeze,
While rabbits play chess beneath leafy peas.

Gnomes in top hats crack jokes on the run,
Chasing fireflies, oh isn't it fun?
Mushrooms are hats on a snail's tiny head,
While hedgehogs do tango, just like we said.

Sunbeams wink through the branches above,
Breezy balloons float with laughter and love.
Each leaf a story, each branch a tune,
In this whimsical place, where smiles are strewn.

A picnic spread out on mossy old stones,
Singing with critters, no need for phones.
Cake made of twigs and a drink of fresh dew,
In the forest's embrace, life starts anew.

Celestial Dance of the Woodlands

The stars at night wear hats of bright light,
Owls with ties keep the woodland in sight.
Fireflies flicker, they start a soirée,
Where trees burst with laughter, come join the ballet!

Dancing through shadows, a fox in attire,
Fallen leaves dance, setting the woods on fire.
Mice dress in wool, they chatter and cheer,
While the moon nods along, oh my dear, oh dear!

Balloons on branches, a funny sight here,
A raccoon in socks sips soda and beer.
With each little twirl, there's a giggle, a squeak,
Nature's own party, go join the mystique!

As dawn slowly stretches, the night bids adieu,
Yet the whispers continue, they're waiting for you.
Laughs echo softly through each forest stream,
Life here is silly, it's all a big dream.

Twilight Reveries in the Pines

When twilight paints skies a candy-floss hue,
Pine trees wear capes made of glimmering dew.
Crickets are DJs, and squirrels take the stage,
With rhythm so catchy, it's all the rage!

Bees buzz like drummers in silly old hats,
While raccoons and badgers engage in their chats.
Shadows do waltzes, they swish and they sway,
In the heart of the woods, we merrily play.

Stars start to wink, they're up for a cheer,
As bunnies recite tales from yesteryear.
Laughter rings out as a bear takes a shot,
At trying to dance, oh what a funny plot!

A picnic of berries and cheese just for fun,
Under sparkling starlight, we're never done.
Each moment is magic, each grin is a gleam,
In this twilight world, we're lost in a dream.

Shimmering Pathways of Lost Dreams

On pathways that shimmer like golden thread,
Newt scholars debate what the crickets have said.
Rabbits with glasses ponder the lore,
While hedgehogs ride scooters and laugh by the shore.

Feathers and sparkles make up their attire,
Bushes are stages for acts to inspire.
Ducks in a conga line waddle with glee,
Singing of wishes, oh so wild and free!

The breeze it carries a mischievous tune,
While trees sway and chuckle beneath the full moon.
Pine cones in hand, they gather for games,
Making up jokes with the silliest names.

As twilight deepens and dreams intertwine,
Each shared laugh a thread in this tapestry fine.
In this land of wonder, where giggles take flight,
Lost dreams are found in the soft, starry night.

Enchanted Ferns and Flickering Stars

Underneath the dancing trees,
The squirrels wear tiny tees,
They form a band, all in a row,
Singing songs, oh what a show!

Fairies giggle by the brook,
Reading fortunes from a book,
With every page, the pages flip,
Creating magic with each quip.

Mushrooms wear their finest hats,
They host parties for the cats,
Who sip tea from acorn cups,
As nightfall tickles sleepy pups.

And as the stars blink back their glee,
The fireflies join in on the spree,
With jokes that twinkle through the night,
Oh, what a whimsical delight!

Emerald Visions on Twilight Paths

In the glade where shadows creep,
Toadstools shout, 'Come take a leap!'
Fairy lights twirl in the air,
While chipmunks debate about their hair.

A wise old owl can't quite see,
He misplaces his cup of tea,
While crickets play their jazzy tunes,
And raccoons dance beneath the moons.

The trees all whisper with delight,
As otters giggle, oh, what a sight!
With pinecones flying like confetti,
They celebrate the days all petty.

Each laugh echoes through the night,
As shadows join the playful fight,
Beneath the stars, the fun's aglow,
In magic realms where giggles flow!

Celestial Foliage and Serene Nights

On starlit nights, the leaves conspire,
To form a band, with great desire,
A melody of rustling cheer,
That brings the critters gathered near.

Mice don hats and tap dance by,
While owls hoot, 'Oh me, oh my!'
With every step, the grasses sway,
As shadows prance and hearts display.

Fireflies flash their disco lights,
Twinkling bright on cozy nights,
While napping bears play silly dreams,
Of dancing cheese and chocolate streams.

The foliage giggles with great mirth,
As crickets share their comedic worth,
In this enchanted, leafy scene,
Where laughter reigns and all's serene!

Mystic Horizons of Spruce and Cedar

In a wood where secrets nest,
Spruce and cedar wear their best,
Squirrels juggle acorns high,
While bluebirds chat, oh my, oh my!

Gnomes in hats that tip and sway,
Tell funny tales of yesterday,
Climbing branches with a grin,
As raccoons cheer and join in.

The shadows play hide-and-seek,
While owls chat and softly peek,
With stories shared in moonlit glades,
Where laughter floats on gentle raids.

In this realm of sprucy cheer,
Every critter sings sincere,
With dreams that sparkle, bounce, and beam,
In this woodland, all's a dream!

Milton Keynes UK
Ingram Content Group UK Ltd.
UKHW021948151124
451186UK00007B/158

9 789916 943861